The Great Gift of Ghee

Dedication

*Like Ghee, the recipes in this book are an ode to the
ancestors. A salute to the intuitive foresight and mindful
sensitivity that comes effortlessly to people who are
attuned to the natural rhythms of this universe.*

Contents

Fall

Winter

Spice Blends

Pickles & Chutneys

NOTES ON GHEE

Ghee is very easy to use.
Experiment with it and incorporate it
into your daily routine.

A letter from the author

My personal journey with Ghee began after I had three baby boys, two years apart, in a span of four years.

Already in my early thirties, amidst the challenges of new motherhood on one hand and immeasurable happiness on the other, the natural instinct to provide an environment of nurture for the babies became paramount. I found myself searching for the best foods that tradition had to offer and rediscovered Ghee!

Until the mid-1900s, Ghee was a homemade specialty and very precious. It was made in small batches and used for foods prepared as *prasadam*, or offerings on holy days, and sometimes as a treat on freshly cooked, hot foods. Although I don't remember it being everyday fare, school friends from more traditional homes say it was always available in a small stainless steel container on the dining table. This utensil, called a Ghee-*daani* resembles a jam-pot. One simply dipped a small spoon in and added a dollop of Ghee to freshly cooked, steaming hot food. A favorite lunch in a typical Maharashtrian home is *varan-bhaat-ani-toop*, literally lentils boiled with turmeric and served with rice and Ghee!

I slowly started incorporating Ghee into the food for my young children. A spoonful in the rice. A few drops on their *chapatis*. A drizzle over their afternoon bowl of lentils. Never too much. But always with the conviction that it made a difference.

At that time, I had no idea about its scientific benefits. For me, Ghee in those days was unique and special, it was simply a trusted traditional gift, handed down for generations.

There are many verses in the *Vedas*, the ancient spiritual texts from India, that extol the virtues of Ghee. It is repeatedly mentioned and associated with a superior existence. In fact, later when out of curiosity, I started researching Ghee, I realized that centuries ago, it was only available to the privileged. To those who had access to the milk of single humped cows, indigenous to the Indian subcontinent.

Native Indic cows have the *Surya-Ketu-Nadi* referring to their single hump. *Surya* is a synonym for the Sun, *Ketu* refers to one of the Lunar Nodes in Vedic Astrology and *Nadi* is derived from the Sanskrit root word *nad* meaning channel or flow. So it all makes sense that these cows are cared for with such reverence and the Ghee is usually made around the full-moon or every 28 days.

In 2008 when I moved to Los Angeles with the children, I was fortunate to meet Susanne, the co-publisher on this project. She had never been to India, but was already making Ghee at home from organic, unsalted, sweet cream butter and experimenting with a few Indian recipes. Susanne opened up her kitchen to me and together we started on a cooking journey.

While sharing all the recipes I had watched traditional cooks make in India, the fascinating revelations of Ghee became evident. It is truly a superfood in every sense. Adding nutrition and flavor to all things savory or sweet, it has now become a mainstay in our kitchens.

Susanne went further, and has now visited India several times. She has done Panchkarma, which is a special Ayurvedic cleanse and rejuvenation technique spanning approximately four weeks. One of the procedures during Panchkarma, requires one to drink prescribed amounts of medicated Ghee, under a doctor's supervision.

The recipes are divided into seasonal groups keeping in mind the cooling and warming potential of different foods. Nevertheless, feel free to mix and match them to suit your own lifestyle. Eating fresh and locally available foods, whenever possible, is the secret to good health. Also, while trying out these recipes, remember that the level of salt, sweetness and heat can be adjusted to suit your palate.

My children are now 26, 24, and 22 years old. The need to share all that I've learned while cooking for them and watching them grow into strong young men is compelling. And Ghee has become a key ingredient that encapsulates my world of comfort foods. Whether I make an all Indian meal, a quintessential English pie or a quick batch of muffins, Ghee makes me feel at home wherever I am!

If you have not experimented with Ghee or Indian cuisine before, these simple and delicious recipes are a good starting point. Having taught them to many friends in Los Angeles, I know that you too will be able to master them effortlessly. Begin with half a spoonful on a hot steaming bowl of oats.

As an ancient saying in Sanskrit somewhat goes, "no matter how you procure the Ghee, make sure you eat a little bit every day!"

Chitra Martin

Ghee is a sublime and unique butter fat.

The original recipe for Ghee is several thousand years old. References to it are found in most spiritual and epic texts in Sanskrit, one of the oldest proto-Indo-European languages, that is still alive in India.

Traditionally, Ghee is the pure, saturated fat that is collected after boiling down full fat butter made from yoghurt-cream, which in turn is made from fresh whole milk, until all the moisture has evaporated and all the milk solids have settled at the bottom. Leaving pure, saturated, clarified Ghee.

Another method that has recently gained popularity is that of slowly heating unsalted, sweet-cream butter to achieve a similar result. The former procedure can be more expensive and time consuming, so many of us opt for the latter in our home kitchens, for the sake of convenience.

In Ayurveda, the ancient practice of healing with the help of herbs, spices, massages and cleanses, the yoghurt-cream-butter method of making Ghee is used. The milk source for Ghee ideally ought to be the nutrient-rich, "A2-type" milk, derived from the single humped cows native to India.

Over thousands of years of everyday use, Ghee has proved to have tremendous healing and restorative qualities. In the Sanskrit Ayurvedic texts, it is mentioned that Ghee has the ability to permeate the organs and muscles, softening them and drawing out the toxins from the system. Pure Ghee has a distinct taste. It either tastes like a deep, rich cheese if extracted from the yoghurt butter fat or has a delicious, nutty, slightly caramelized flavor if derived from organic, grass-fed sweet-cream butter.

The taste may vary depending on the cooking process used. Both types of Ghee are completely free of sugars, salt and milk proteins. Both are pure and clarified.

Like many other indigenous foods, Ghee has recently come into the global culinary limelight.

In the wake of scientific research for better health care, Ghee is now widely accepted as a good fat that helps us avoid the after-effects of processed, unhealthy fats.

This book, and all it offers is our way of saying 'thank you' to our ancestors for this great gift of Ghee that transcends every oil or butter in its nutritious goodness and delicious flavor.

Essentials in your pantry

PANS

TAWA: A light-weight iron griddle with a handle: Called a *Tawa* in Hindi, it is usually concave, but can also be flat. Used to make *Chapatis*, *Parathas*, and *Dosas*.

SAUCEPANS: Must be heavy bottom preferably stainless steel, with fitting lids.

CHAKLA BELAN: Rolling pin and flat circular rolling board.

SPICE GRINDER: Helps while grinding hard spices like cinnamon, cardamom, cloves, whole black pepper.

KADHAI: Indian style wok. Usually made of iron or heavy stainless steel, it is flatter than a Chinese wok and easy to handle. Its shape lends itself perfectly for traditional Indian stir fried dishes.

SPICES

SEEDS: cumin, coriander, mustard, nigella, fennel, and fenugreek

POWDERS: turmeric, cumin, coriander, red chili, asafetida, and black salt

Black Salt, also called kala-namak in Hindi, is a naturally occurring rock salt that has high contents of phosphorus and sodium sulfide. It has a strong flavor and is widely used in Asia. It is cooling and acts as a digestive.

HERBS

FRESH HERBS: cilantro, mint, fenugreek leaves, dill, and curry leaves

Curry Leaves or Kari Leaves, whichever way you spell them, are unique to Indian cuisine. The dark green and aromatic leaves are rich in magnesium, copper, iron, calcium, phosphorus and vitamins A, B and E. They also contain essential amino acids and glycosides.

DRIED HERBS: bay leaves, fenugreek leaves, cinnamon, cloves, cardamom

FATS

GHEE: Made from yoghurt-butter-cream or from regular unsalted butter.

OILS: sesame, coconut, refined peanut, mustard, and sunflower

SWEETENER

JAGGERY: A concentrated form of sugar cane juice. It is also made from the sap of date palms.

In Indian cuisine, jaggery is used to balance the salt according to the guidelines of Ayurveda, which recommends that all six tastes be included in a complete meal. Jaggery is rich in natural minerals like zinc and selenium.

Ghee *Tadka*: a unique form of tempering

Unique to Indian cuisine, the term Tadka translates as tempering with hot oil or Ghee.

Besides adding a delicious twist, the popping and crackling of whole spices and seeds in hot Ghee releases their essential nutrients, enhancing the nutritional value of a *Tadka*.

A typical *Tadka*:

♦ *Heat 1 ½–2 tbsp of Ghee, add ½ tsp mustard seeds, allow them to crackle and pop. Lower the heat to medium.*

♦ *Then, in quick succession, add cumin seeds, asafetida, a dash of salt, dried red chilies or green chilies, curry leaves, ginger and garlic.*

♦ *Allow the ingredients to sizzle and cook for a full minute, swirling them around constantly.*

♦ *Add this sizzling mix or Tadka to any cooked lentil, basic soup, cooked rice or even steamed vegetables. Stir or toss—and voila—you have an Indian entrée!*

Ghee, mustard seeds, cumin seeds, and asafetida are the most common components of a typical *Tadka*. However, you can choose any combination from the ingredients mentioned here, or add a few whole spices like black pepper, bay leaves, cinnamon, cardamom and cloves to the mix.

A *Tadka* is usually still sizzling and smoking when it is added to a simmering lentil or entrée. However, there are a few hot *Tadkas* that are added to room temperature liquids, to cold salads and sometimes even cooled down completely and then later, added to pickles.

Kitchen Tip:

To make a delicious Raita, add a Tadka of mustard seeds, curry leaves, and white lentils to a bowl of whipped yoghurt. Add finely chopped cucumber, salt, and a dash of sugar.

BEGINNING
WITH GHEE

Here are a few super simple recipes
for anyone who has not used Ghee before.

If you are using Ghee for the first time

- Ghee has a high smoking point : 485°F or 252°C.

- Ghee does not necessarily require additional heating. It can be added at the beginning as part of the tempering, in the middle or at the end of a recipe as in a smoothie, or a spoonful on hot food.

- Ghee and Sesame Oil are the oldest forms of oils or fats known since ancient times and are still the healthiest options for cooking today.

- Ghee and milk from tenderly cared for, hand-milked, Indian cows, whose calves get their mother's milk first, is traditionally regarded nutritionally on par with human milk.

- Ghee made from the milk of native Indic cows is rich in nutrients and has Omega 3 and Omega 9, vitamins A, D, E and K.

- Ghee also has Butyric Acid, an essential ingredient that ensures balance in the gut.

- Ghee is usually a light or dark golden colored liquid, depending on the duration for which the butter has been slow cooked.

- Ghee may solidify at lower temperatures but will melt easily when warmed, without any changes in its essence or nutrients.

- Ghee does not require refrigeration and has a long shelf life.

- Stored at room temperature, a good quality Ghee can be used for over six to eight months and sometimes even longer. Ayurvedic tradition even has external "medicinal" applications for long-aged Ghee, that have been used by multiple generations of a family!

- Ghee and butter cannot be substituted for each other in all recipes. However, one could successfully use Ghee in place of butter when sautéing vegetables and meats and in certain desserts. We suggest you follow a few recipes initially and then experiment with it yourself.

- Ghee is very versatile and can be used as a topical balm for minor burns and skin eruptions.

- Ghee holds a very special place in Ayurveda. It is used as a part of the process called Panchakarma, which is a total cleanse. The recipient, under professional supervision, drinks a prescribed amount of Ghee that has been infused with medicinal herbs to help eliminate stubborn toxins from the system.

- Ghee is traditionally made from milk of native Indic cows, but it can also be made from other kinds, like buffalo or goat milk.

Homemade Ghee

Making Ghee at home is easy once you've watched someone do it a couple of times.
There are several tutorial videos on the internet that will help you through the process!

Approximately
One 16 oz Jar

2 lbs organic, unsalted, full
fat, sweet cream butter (or
any unsalted, good quality,
full fat butter)

Cookware:

heavy bottom saucepan
ladle
cheese cloth or paper filter
ceramic or glass jar

Put the butter into a saucepan over low heat. Initially, stir it a few times until all the butter has melted. Once the butter melts, make sure the heat is very low. Allow this to cook until it is bubbling. Do not stir it anymore.

With a ladle, carefully remove some of the foam that accumulates on top.

Ultimately, after 30 to 40 minutes, all the moisture will have evaporated and there will be a clear liquid in the pan. Once the residual milk solids become reddish brown, it's time to take it off the heat.

Allow it to stand for 10 minutes before passing it through a filter into a jar.

Ghee should cool completely before closing the lid of the jar. Store in a cool, dry place on the kitchen counter or in a cabinet. Keep away from direct sunlight.

Kitchen Tip: *Ghee does not need refrigeration since it is a highly saturated fat. It keeps well on the counter or on a shelf for a very long time.*

Broken Wheat Porridge

This is a very simple porridge, nourishing and hearty. But you can jazz it up with roasted nuts, raisins or any fruits of your choice to make it a perfect breakfast bowl.

Serves
2 Medium Portions

1 cup broken wheat

3 whole green cardamoms

4 – 5 whole black peppercorns

2 tbsp Ghee

½ tsp Himalayan pink salt or sea salt

hot water as required

Cookware:

deep, heavy saucepan with handle

ladle to stir

Wash and soak the broken wheat for 1 hour in 1 ½ cups of hot water. In a mortar pestle or on a chopping board, roughly pound the green cardamoms and whole peppercorns. In a heavy saucepan with a handle, add 1 ½ tbsp Ghee. Heat on high, and then lower the heat to medium low. Add the cardamom and pepper.

Lift the saucepan an inch away from the heat and swirl for a few seconds until aromatic. Do not let the delicate spices burn. Add the soaked and drained broken wheat. Stir fry for 2 minutes, on medium heat, without browning the broken wheat kernels.

When the wheat is just a shade darker, add 4 cups of very hot water slowly, lowering the heat as you go along. Be very careful as it will sizzle and splutter.

Stir well and add ½ tsp sea salt or Himalayan pink salt. Turn the heat up and bring to a boil on medium – low. Cook for 30 to 45 minutes, until the wheat is mushy and soft. Adjust the consistency according to your preference. Add water if too thick, cook further if too thin.

Take off from heat and add the remaining ½ tsp of Ghee. Mix well and serve immediately.

Kitchen Tip:

Broken wheat porridge thickens on cooling. So if you refrigerate any leftovers, be sure to add a little hot water or milk when reheating it. Vegans can also enjoy this porridge with almond or coconut milk.

Rava Upama Spicy wheat semolina

Rich in protein, vitamin B6 and iron, wheat semolina is a popular grain in many parts of the world. A nourishing bowl of rava upama is easy to rustle up and requires minimal prep.

Serves
2 Large Portions

1 cup *rava* (wheat semolina)

1 small onion, cut fine

½ tsp mustard seeds

1 tbsp *urad daal* (white lentils)

10–12 curry leaves

1 inch fresh ginger root, grated

small bunch cilantro, washed and cut fine

1½ tbsp cashew nuts

2 tbsp grated coconut

juice of 1 lime

salt

2 tbsp Ghee, divided

2 green chilies, slit or cut fine

Cookware:
large wok
saucepan to boil water

Dry roast the semolina for 6–8 minutes, until a shade darker and aromatic. Remove to a bowl and reserve.

Heat 3 cups of water in a saucepan, until boiling. Keep on low heat to simmer.

In a large wok, heat 1 tbsp Ghee. Fry the cashew nuts for a few minutes until aromatic and slightly pink. Remove and reserve on a plate.

In the same Ghee, add the mustard seeds and white lentils. Allow the mustard to splutter and pop. Add the white lentils and sauté until roasted. This may take a minute or less. Add curry leaves, ginger, onions, salt and green chilies. Stir fry for 2–3 minutes on low to medium heat. The onions should be translucent and slightly pink.

Carefully add the simmering water to the onions and spices. Bring to a boil and check the salt. Cover and allow the mix to simmer for 5–7 minutes. This step allows the onions to soften and the ginger to cook thoroughly. Add half the lime juice and the remaining tbsp of Ghee.

Lower the heat, and slowly add the roasted semolina, stirring constantly. Make sure all the semolina, hot water and spices come together well.

Add half the cleaned and cut cilantro at this stage. Cover and steam on low heat for 6–8 minutes.

Fluff with a fork, garnish with remaining cilantro, grated coconut, fried cashew nuts and lime juice. Serve immediately.

Kitchen Tip: *The addition of green peas makes this a hearty meal. Feel free to add another teaspoon of Ghee while serving.*

Akuri Bombay style, spicy scrambled eggs

Akuri is a popular breakfast, but it also makes the best instant dinner after a busy and long work day.

Serves
3 Medium Portions

4 large eggs

2 tbsp Ghee

1 medium onion

1 green chili, finely diced

1 tsp coarsely ground black pepper, divided

½ tsp turmeric powder

2 small, juicy, ripe tomatoes

small bunch cilantro leaves, divided

salt

Cookware:
large wok or a wide-rimmed cooking pan

Lightly beat the eggs with a little salt and keep aside. Separately, dice the onions, tomatoes, green chili and cilantro as fine as possible.

Heat the Ghee in a wok or wide-rimmed pan. Add half the coarsely ground black pepper and simmer for a few seconds. Add the finely diced green chili and fry for a few seconds.

Add the onion. Fry on high heat, stirring constantly, until the onions are golden brown. Lower heat to medium. Add salt, turmeric and one third of the chopped cilantro.

After a minute, add the finely diced tomatoes and cook on medium heat until the Ghee separates and the tomatoes are soft. Add another one-third of cilantro. Add the eggs and fold into the spicy onion – tomato mixture.

Allow the eggs to cook, while stirring, making sure you pick up all the egg from the base as you go along. Keep mixing and folding until the eggs have cooked and are well mixed.

Check the salt. Add the remaining cilantro and black pepper. Serve hot with freshly toasted bread and butter.

Kitchen Tip:
There are a few different versions of this quick and easy meal. You can add ingredients like garlic and coarsely ground cumin while frying the onions. Or leave out the tomatoes. It's versatile and adaptable.

Sautéed Seasonal Vegetables

Serves
2 Medium Portions

1 ½ cups of your favorite vegetable combination in bite sized pieces (green beans, carrots, broccoli, cauliflower, potatoes, asparagus, sweet potato, bell peppers, onions)

½ tsp cumin seeds

¼ tsp turmeric powder

½ tsp red chili flakes (optional)

2 garlic flakes – chopped fine or ground

1 tbsp Ghee

juice of 1 lemon

¼ cup washed and drained cilantro – use the leaves and very tender stalks

Cookware:
skillet that is 2 inches deep
ladle or wooden spoon to stir

If you prep a few of your favorite vegetables in advance, this is such an easy dinner to rustle up! You could also use a single vegetable – instead of a combination. One of my favorite variations is asparagus sautéed in Ghee, a crushed garlic clove and a dash of red chili flakes, drizzle with lemon juice and enjoy.

Boil or blanch the vegetables as needed – they should be cooked and edible.

Root vegetables like sweet potato or yams should be cooked separately. Beans, carrots, broccoli and cauliflower can be blanched in boiling water for 3 minutes and then rinsed with cold water to retain their crunch.

Bell peppers and onions should only be sliced or diced.

In a skillet, heat 1 tbsp Ghee. Add cumin and swirl for a few seconds. Add the garlic, stir it around for half a minute or so. Do not brown the garlic.

While sizzling, add the vegetables and stir for 2 minutes on high heat. Add the salt, turmeric and chili flakes. Stir for another 2 minutes.

Remove from heat.

Pour half the lemon juice over the vegetables. Add half the chopped cilantro – toss. Garnish with remaining cilantro. Serve with lemon juice on the side.

 Kitchen Tip: *This recipe is great with frozen vegetables too. Just make sure you run the vegetables under warm water for a minute before adding them to a hot skillet, so they start thawing immediately. If you need the carbs pile it up on a bed of cooked rice!*

Basic Khichadi Everyday rice and lentil cooked together

Serves
3 Medium Portions

¼ cup white Basmati rice

¼ cup yellow mung lentils

¼ cup mixed vegetables
(optional)

1 tbsp + ½ tsp Ghee

salt

1 green chili, slit in two

½ tsp turmeric powder

¼ tsp cumin seeds

1 inch piece cinnamon

2 green cardamoms, split open

3 cloves

1 bay leaf

6–7 whole black peppercorns

1 inch piece freshly grated
ginger root

Cookware:
large, deep saucepan with a
handle and a fitting lid

The very definition of a Khichadi is a 'one-pot-meal' where a list of ingredients have been put together in a sequence to create a single entrée! Commonly made with whole grains, lentils, spices and herbs, recipes for Khichadis can vary by region, by season and by choice.

The best part about this Khichadi is you can choose the ingredients. Except for the lentils, rice and Ghee, everything else on the list is optional! So if you don't have some ingredients, use the others, and you will still enjoy a bowl of amazing goodness. Or, for a more complete meal, add a bowl of steamed vegetables on top of the basic Khichadi and enjoy it as a healthy option.

Wash the rice and lentils together and soak in a cup of water for half an hour.

In a heavy saucepan, heat 1 tbsp Ghee. Add the cumin, cardamom, cinnamon, cloves, whole peppercorns, bay leaf. Lower the heat slightly and swirl them around. Add the green chili and freshly grated ginger root.

Add the drained rice and lentil mix. Stir for 2 minutes, until fragrant.

Add 3 cups hot water, salt, and turmeric. Stir and bring to a full boil. Lower heat and cook covered until done. This Khichadi usually has a porridge like consistency and should not become too dry. Check the seasoning and add salt if need be. Serve hot with the remaining ½ tsp of Ghee.

Kitchen Tip: *Khichadi is the perfect homemade meal. You can prep the ingredients in the morning – come home after a long day at work and put it together in under an hour!*

SEASONAL RECIPES

Indian cuisine recommends that we
eat seasonal vegetables and use locally
grown herbs and spices.

Also, remember, Ghee is always used
in moderation. Even traditional cooks
only use a little Ghee to make the food
nutritious and delicious.

Spring Menu

Daliya Khichadi
Broken wheat with vegetables

Sambar
Spicy lentils with vegetables

Coconut Rice

Rasam
Spicy broth with lemon

Mixed Vegetables

Chapatis
plain bread

Aloo Paratha
Bread stuffed with spiced potatoes

Magas
Chickpea flour and Ghee dessert

Daliya Khichadi Broken wheat with vegetables

Serves
3 Large Portions

½ cup bulgur or broken wheat

½ cup yellow mung *daal* (lentils)

1 green chili, ground to a coarse paste with 1 ½ inch piece fresh ginger

1½ cups of diced vegetables (carrots, green beans, cauliflower, peas, potatoes – or a combination of any three)

salt

4 tbsp Ghee

4 cloves

2 green cardamoms

1 two-inch piece of cinnamon

1 tbsp freshly roasted, ground coriander seeds

1 tsp cumin seeds

½ tbsp crushed black peppercorns

½ tsp asafetida

½ tsp turmeric powder

1 tsp red chili powder (or as per taste)

Cookware:
2 quart, heavy bottom, deep saucepan

This Khichadi is just wonderful served by itself on a cool, crisp Spring day. It's like an entire meal in a bowl, and will leave you feeling nourished and warm from within. Try it with a scoop of sweetened yoghurt and your favorite crisps.

Wash and drain the broken wheat along with the Mung *Daal*, leaving very little water in the bowl. Let it stand for half an hour.

Heat 3 tbsp Ghee in heavy bottom, deep saucepan. Add the 4 cloves, 2 green cardamoms, 1 two-inch piece of cinnamon. Lower the heat to medium.

Add cumin, half the crushed black pepper, asafetida and fry for a few seconds. Add the green chilies and ginger paste. Stir for a few seconds.

Add the crushed coriander seeds, red chili powder and turmeric. Lower the heat to minimum.

Add the mixed broken wheat and mung lentils. Stir on medium heat for 4 minutes. Add all the vegetables. Stir for another 2 or 3 minutes on medium high.

Add 3 cups water and cook for 20 minutes. This Khichadi should have the consistency of a thick porridge. If it gets too dry, add ½ a cup of boiling water and mix well.

Cook through until done. Garnish with a tablespoon of hot Ghee, the remaining coarse black pepper and a little coriander powder.

Sambar Spicy lentils with vegetables

Serves
4 Medium Portions

1 cup *toor daal* (pigeon peas lentil) boiled and mashed

1 cup mixed vegetables diced: potato, carrots, beans, drumsticks (fruit of the moringa plant) and baby-eggplant

1 small onion, cubed

6 baby shallots, peeled

3 dried red chilies

1 lemon sized ball of tamarind soaked in 1 cup boiling water for half an hour

2 tbsp Ghee

1 tsp mustard seeds

1 tsp cumin seeds

¼ tsp fenugreek seeds

½ tsp asafetida

4 garlic flakes, crushed

1 small tomato

10 fresh curry leaves

½ cup coconut milk

1 tbsp jaggery or brown sugar

½ tsp turmeric powder

1 tsp ready made *sambar* powder (pg 94)

Cookware:

3 quart, heavy bottom saucepan with fitting lid

This is a fairly thick soup that is made all year round but tastes wonderful in Spring when all the vegetables are available. It is served with rice, or fermented and steamed rice cakes (idlis), crepes made with a variety of batters (dosas) and sometimes with deep fried, spicy lentil fritters shaped like doughnuts (medu-vadas).

Sambar is South India's comfort food that is now popular all over the country and the world. Every person you meet will claim that nobody makes it like their own favorite home-cook. It is spicy, tangy, nourishing and a filling soup by itself. Over freshly steamed Basmati rice, it is even better.

Heat Ghee in a heavy saucepan. Add the mustard seeds and allow them to pop. Add the asafetida and dried red chilies – swirl around for a few seconds. Add the curry leaves.

Add in quick succession: the cumin seeds, fenugreek seeds, garlic, turmeric and red chili powder. After a few seconds, add the vegetables along with the chopped tomatoes. Mix well and add the tamarind extract, squeezing all the juice.

Add ½ cup coconut milk. Add your own homemade Sambar powder and salt. Add the jaggery.

Add 1 ½ cups of warm water. Cover and cook for 10 minutes, until the vegetables are almost done.

Add the cooked and mashed *toor daal* – adjusting the consistency with a little hot water if needed. Simmer for another 10 minutes until fragrant and cooked through.

Taste for salt, jaggery, chili powder – adding some if needed.

Coconut Rice

Coconuts are complete foods. They have all the goodness of iron, potassium, manganese and vitamin B6. High in caloric content, they are a storehouse of energy. Although ancient cultures have used organic coconut oil for thousands of years, it is once again being recognized as a superfood and is now recommended as part of many healthy diets. Combined with Ghee and some essential spices, a bowl of coconut rice makes a complete meal on a bright, Spring day.

Serves
4 Medium Portions

1 cup basmati rice
washed and drained in a sieve

1 cup thick coconut milk, fresh or instant

1 ¼ cup warm water

2 tbsp cashew nuts

3 tbsp coconut flakes, dry roasted until pink

2 dry red chilies

2 green chilies

½ tsp coarsely crushed black pepper

1 inch piece cinnamon

1 star anise

5 green cardamoms

1 tsp black peppercorns

2 bay leaves

7 cloves

½ tsp mustard seeds

½ tsp cumin seeds

1½ inch piece grated ginger root

10 curry leaves

2 tbsp Ghee

1 tsp salt

small bunch cilantro, chopped fine

Cookware:
heavy bottom, 2 quart sauce-pan with fitting lid

Heat Ghee in a heavy bottom, deep saucepan, and fry the cashews until pink. Drain and reserve them on a plate.

In the same pan add cinnamon, cloves, cardamom, bay leaves, star anise, peppercorns and dry red chilies. Allow them to sizzle. Add ½ tsp mustard seeds and allow them to pop.

After a few seconds add the cumin seeds and stir for a few seconds. Add grated ginger, green chilies and fresh curry leaves. Tear the curry leaves into a few pieces to release their aroma.

Fry these ingredients on medium heat, but do not allow them to burn. Add the washed and drained rice and stir very carefully so that the delicate basmati rice does not break.

After 2 minutes, add 1 full cup coconut milk and some salt. Add 2 tbsp of the roasted coconut flakes, reserve 1 tbsp for the final garnish. Stir once and lower heat.

Now add 1 ¼ cup warm water. Stir and allow it to simmer on low to medium heat. Once the moisture is almost dry, add half the chopped cilantro.

Check the salt and add more if required. Lower heat to minimum. Cover and cook until the rice is done.

Fluff the rice with a fork before serving and garnish with roasted coconut flakes, cilantro and fried cashews.

Rasam Spicy broth with lemon

Rasam is an excellent digestive. In a typical South Indian home, it is usually the soup du jour. Many like it extra hot and spicy, so adjust the level of heat with the number of red chilies and black pepper powder.

Serves
4 Medium Portions

½ cup yellow mung *daal*, washed and soaked for an hour

juice of 2 lemons

½ cup cilantro

1 tbsp Ghee

1 tsp turmeric powder

½ tsp mustard seeds

½ tsp cumin seeds

½ tsp asafetida

10–15 fresh curry leaves

2 inch piece of freshly grated ginger root

2 green chilies

¼ cup freshly grated or frozen coconut

2 dried red chilies

1 tsp coarsely ground black pepper

Cookware:
2 quart deep saucepan for the Rasam

round and deep serving spoon

small skillet for the tempering or *Tadka*

Boil the yellow mung *daal* in 1 ½ cups of water, with salt and turmeric until completely cooked and mushy. The water will evaporate, so cook on high heat until boiling and then reduce to medium low until done.

Add 3 cups of hot water to get a broth like consistency. Reserve a handful of cilantro for the garnish, and add the rest to the simmering *daal*. Add half the freshly grated ginger root. Add the finely chopped green chilies and grated coconut. Allow the *daal* with the additional water to simmer for 5 – 7 minutes.

While the *daal* is simmering, prepare the tempering in a small skillet. Heat the Ghee. Add the mustard seeds and allow them to pop. Add the asafetida, remaining grated ginger root, fresh curry leaves, dried red chilies and coarsely ground black pepper.

Carefully swirl it around for a few seconds so that all the ingredients are well fried in the hot Ghee. While it's still sizzling – add it to the simmering Rasam. Take off from the heat.

Add half the lemon juice and check the level of sourness. Check the salt.

Correct seasoning, adding more lemon juice if required.

Allow it to stand for 5 minutes. Serve it with the remaining lemon juice in a bowl on the side.

Kitchen Tip: *The grated coconut is a traditional ingredient. You could leave it out if unavailable.*

Mixed Vegetables Green beans / carrots / zucchini / peas

Serves
4 Medium Portions

2 cups mixed vegetables, cut into bite size pieces

3 medium red or brown onions, chopped fine

3 medium tomatoes, chopped fine

3 tbsp Ghee

2 green chilies, chopped fine

1 tsp cumin seeds

1 tsp turmeric

2 tbsp freshly roasted and coarsely ground coriander seeds

1 tsp freshly ground cumin powder

1 tsp mild red chili powder

1 ¾ tsp *garam masala* powder (pg 91)

1½ tbsp ginger-garlic paste (preferably fresh and coarsely ground)

1 tsp salt

¼ tsp sugar

½ cup fresh cilantro – washed and chopped fine

Cookware:

skillet that is 2 inches deep

ladle or wooden spoon to stir

Without the vegetables, this recipe makes an excellent 'base-sauce' that is very popular in North India. It can even be made in advance and frozen in small batches. Just sauté a few vegetables in Ghee and add the 'base-sauce' for an interesting variation.

Heat Ghee in a heavy wok or skillet. Add the cumin seeds and lower heat to medium.

Add the chopped onions when the cumin turns a shade darker. Add ¼ tsp salt, to release the water content in the onions. Fry over medium heat, until the onions are a rich, golden brown. Add the ginger-garlic paste. Keep stirring on medium heat, until fragrant and brown.

When the Ghee separates, add the cumin, coriander, turmeric and chili powders. Stir well. Do not let the spices burn. Splash a few sprinkles of water if necessary. Add 1 tsp Garam Masala at this stage. Regulate the heat between medium and low as you work on slow cooking the mixture.

Add the tomatoes and lower heat. Cover and cook until all the tomatoes have broken down to a pulp and the mix begins to resemble a thick sauce. Add ¼ cup hot water and simmer for another 10 minutes or until the Ghee separates from the mixture.

Add the mixed vegetables, stir well to coat them with the onion and tomato sauce.

Simmer on medium to low heat until vegetables are cooked through. Add ¼ tsp sugar, mix again. Sprinkle the remaining ½ tsp Garam Masala. Cover and cook on the lowest possible heat for another minute. Taste for salt and adjust if required.

 Kitchen Tip: *You can either leave it thick or add some vegetable stock and make the gravy thinner. Make sure you adjust the salt and chili according to the stock added.*

Chapatis Flat, unleavened bread

Serves
4 Chapatis

1½ cups whole wheat flour
¼ tsp salt
1 tsp melted Ghee
warm water as required

Cookware:

Tawa: flat or slightly concave iron skillet with a handle, light and easy to move around

large, open, mixing bowl to make the dough

light and slim rolling pin

round tortilla box to keep the *chapatis* warm

kitchen towel to line the box

Chapatis are usually made fresh every day. They are served with all meals and make perfect wraps with sautéed vegetables. You can also enjoy them with lentils or gravies.

For the dough: In a large mixing bowl, make a soft dough with the ingredients. Add the warm water, very little at a time, making sure you incorporate all the dry flour and there are no flour-pockets or lumps in the dough.

When it has all come together successfully, put a few drops of Ghee on your hands and knead until smooth. Cover and rest for 20–30 minutes.

After resting the dough for 30 minutes, knead it again for a few minutes. Divide the dough into 4 equal portions.

Roll each portion, one at a time, to approximately 1/10 of an inch thickness, with the help of plain, dry wheat flour. It should resemble a thin tortilla of about 6–8 inches.

Cook one at a time on medium high heat. Baste with Ghee after both sides are almost done. Plain *chapatis* take approximately 2–3 full minutes each to cook.

Kitchen Tip:

Chapatis stay for almost up to a week. The dough keeps well in the refrigerator for 2 days only. We do not recommend keeping chapati dough for longer.

Aloo Paratha Bread stuffed with spiced potatoes

Serves
4 Potato Parathas

For the dough:
2 cups whole wheat flour
¼ tsp salt
1 tsp melted Ghee
warm water as required

Filling for the parathas:
2 boiled potatoes
1 green chili – minced
½ tsp whole cumin
¼ tsp black pepper powder
¼ tsp carom seeds (ajwain)
½ cup cilantro – finely cut
1 tsp raw-mango powder
(amchur)
juice of ½ a lemon
salt
dash of cayenne (or more if you like it hot)
1 tsp freshly roasted and coarsely ground coriander seeds

Cookware:
see *Chapati* (pg 32)

The initial process of making a dough is the same for Chapatis. Both are made with unleavened dough that is rolled out into thin disks, stuffed with a filling or plain, and cooked on a flat or slightly concave iron griddle called a Tawa.

If you don't have a Tawa, use any flat skillet. The cooking time may vary slightly, but the end product will be the same.

Follow steps to make the dough for *Chapatis*.

Filling for the Parathas: Grate the boiled potatoes in a large mixing bowl. Add all the ingredients listed above. Check for seasoning. Adjust the salt and sourness with raw mango powder and lemon juice. Divide into 4 equal-sized portions. Roll into firm balls.

After resting the dough for 30 minutes, knead it again for a few minutes. Make a log from the dough and separate 4 portions of dough, the same size as the balls of potato filling. It is important that the ball of potato filling and the ball of dough be of the same size, to ensure even distribution of the filling.

Now carefully, using a little dry flour, roll a dough ball into a 4–5 inch disk. Place a ball of potato filling in the center and lift the edges of dough to form a sealed pocket, very much like a dumpling, a momo or a wonton.

The end product must be round. Roll out into 7–8 inch disks. Cook on medium/high heat. Do not flip the *Paratha* too soon after putting it on a hot *Tawa* griddle. Wait for tiny bubbles to appear, or wait for the color of the dough to darken a shade, then flip it. Baste with Ghee until both sides have a few brown spots and show signs of being cooked.

Do not rush the process. If you try to cook it too fast, the outside will become crisp and burnt, while the dough inside will stay uncooked.

Kitchen Tip: *Both the Chapatis and Parathas can be made ahead on the day you plan to serve them. Keep them safe in a large round tortilla-box, lined with a clean kitchen towel or some parchment. To reheat, simply put them back on the griddle for a few minutes,, flipping in between.*

Magas Chickpea flour and Ghee dessert

Serves
8–10 Portions
(cut into 2" squares)

1½ cup chickpea flour
½ cup Ghee
½ cup granulated sugar
½ tsp cardamom powder
2 tbsp almonds – chopped
or sliced for garnish

Cookware:
wok or skillet that will give
you enough room to stir the
ingredients comfortably

6 inch round or square,
greased dish

Magas is a treat. Just a small piece of it can transport you to the tables of decadent, privileged royalty in India. It is rich in flavor and actually loaded with protein and good fat that is easily digestible. Remember, it has a very high caloric content, so the key to enjoying Magas is self-control.

Grease a small 6 inch dish, that has raised sides, with a few drops of Ghee. Heat ½ cup Ghee in a heavy wok or skillet. Add the chickpea flour. Roast it on low heat, until aromatic and fairly brown.

Do not leave this, not even for a minute. The chickpea flour will burn. Once it is well roasted, the mixture will become light and foamy. Keep stirring for a minute more.

Take off from the heat and add the sugar. Keep stirring for 5–7 minutes more, on low heat. The sugar will melt at first and then the mixture will start thickening.

Add the cardamom powder and mix well. When the Ghee, flour and sugar mixture starts leaving the sides of the pan and comes together in a homogeneous mass, it is time to set the Magas.

Pour into the greased plate, flatten with the help of the back of a spoon.

Garnish with the chopped almonds. Allow it to cool and set. This may take up to 2 or 3 hours. Cut into squares or diamond shaped bites and serve.

Summer Menu

Yellow Mung Khichadi
Lentils and rice

Dill Daal
Yellow lentils with fresh dill

Lemon Rice

Rasam
Spicy broth with tamarind

Bhindi
Stir fried okra

Naan
Flat bread with all-purpose flour

Sheera
Semolina dessert

Yellow Mung Khichadi Lentils and rice

Serves
2–3 Large Portions

½ cup yellow mung *daal*

½ cup white Basmati rice

½ cup vegetables – green peas, carrots, cauliflower, green beans

½ tsp asafetida

1 tsp cumin seeds

1 inch freshly grated ginger root; 1–2 green chilies

1 large tomato – diced (optional)

¼ cup cilantro leaves, chopped

½ tsp whole black pepper

1 inch piece cinnamon

3 green cardamom pods, opened

4–5 cloves

1 bay leaf

¼ tsp fenugreek seeds

1 tsp turmeric

1½ + 1 tbsp Ghee

salt

Cookware:
2 quart, heavy bottom, deep saucepan

Khichadi, whether simple or complicated, tastes divine when served with a yoghurt raita and a spoonful of homemade lemon, ginger, and fresh turmeric pickle (pg 98).

Wash the rice and mung *daal* together and soak for an hour or so.

In a deep saucepan, heat 1 ½ tbsp Ghee. Add the cinnamon, cloves, green cardamom, bay leaf and whole black pepper. Stir for a few seconds. Add the cumin and fenugreek seeds and let them sizzle. Lower the heat slightly and add the asafetida and grated ginger.

Drain all the water and add the rice and mung *daal*. Stir on high heat for 2 minutes. Add the vegetables and the tomatoes if using. Stir for another minute. Add 4 cups of hot water, turmeric and salt. Check seasoning and adjust.

Cover and cook for 30 to 40 minutes, stirring occasionally. Once it's done, it will have the consistency of a porridge.

Take off from heat and add the cilantro. Mix it in gently. Add 1 tbsp of hot Ghee on top. Serve hot.

Dill Daal Yellow lentils with fresh dill

Serves
4 Medium Portions

small bunch fresh dill, 10–12
stalks, washed, picked and
chopped fine (discard tough
stems)

1 cup spinach (optional)

1½–2 inch piece of ginger
root, grated

1 cup yellow mung *daal*,
washed and soaked for an
hour or more

1–2 green chilies, chopped
fine

1 large tomato, chopped fine

1 tsp turmeric

1 tbsp coriander powder

1 tsp cumin seeds

½ tsp asafetida

salt

3 tbsp Ghee

Cookware:
2 quart, deep saucepan

This daal is usually thick in consistency and tastes great with breads or rice. It's the dill that takes center stage in this recipe, although the Ghee is a very special part of this recipe. It just does not taste the same when cooked with any other oil or fat.

Boil and cook the yellow mung *daal* in fresh water for 30 minutes. The water should not be more than an inch above the level of the lentils to ensure quick and thorough cooking. Half way through the cooking process, add the turmeric and salt.

Once the *daal* is completely cooked, mash it against the side of the pan to a homogeneous soup-like consistency. Keep it simmering on the side, on very low heat, while preparing the seasoning.

In a separate pan or small skillet, heat 2–3 tbsp Ghee. Add the whole cumin, asafetida, green chili and grated ginger root – and swirl or stir it for 30–40 seconds. Add the chopped dill, stir for half a minute. Add the tomatoes and allow them to soften and become mushy. Once the Ghee separates, add the coriander powder and stir on high heat.

Add this sizzling mix to the simmering *daal*. Add the chopped spinach, if using. Stir well. Adjust the consistency by adding ½ cup of boiling water if required. Then taste and adjust salt and chili. Allow it to simmer for 5 minutes on very low heat.

Lemon Rice

Serves
4 Medium Portions

2 cups cooked, cooled and fluffed basmati rice

juice of 1 medium lemon (or a large green-lime)

2 tbsp Ghee

1 inch piece ginger, grated or crushed

1 mild green chili, finely chopped or minced

¼ tsp mustard seeds

1 tsp *channa daal* (split Bengal Gram lentil)

1 tsp *urad daal* (white lentil)

¼ cup raw peanuts (optional)

few fresh curry leaves

¼ tsp asafetida

salt to taste

cayenne pepper to taste

½ tsp turmeric powder

few stalks of fresh cilantro, finely chopped

grated coconut (optional)

Cookware:
large bowl and a heavy bottom deep skillet

Lemon rice is a favorite packed lunch in India. It is light, tangy and refreshing and tastes delicious hot or cold. If you do have leftovers, try not to reheat Lemon Rice as the flavors will change. Just bring to room temperature and enjoy it as a salad with some freshly chopped raw vegetables like cucumbers and baby carrots, and a little more lemon juice and cilantro.

In large bowl or rimmed platter, spread the rice and fluff it so there are no lumps. Sprinkle ½ the lemon juice, ½ the turmeric and a little salt and mix without pressing the rice or breaking the long grains.

In a wok or large deep skillet, heat the Ghee for a minute.

Add the mustard seeds and let them crackle. Turn down the heat. Add asafetida, channa *daal, urad daal*, green chili, ginger and curry leaves. Stir, and make sure the ingredients do not burn.

Add the peanuts, if using. Add the remaining turmeric and quickly add the rice mix. Make sure nothing sticks to the bottom of the wok.

Lower heat, add ¼ cup hot water. Blend gently and steam covered for 5-6 minutes. Uncover and add the remaining lemon juice. Stir, garnish with fresh cilantro and grated coconut.

Rasam Spicy broth with tamarind

Serves
4 Large Portions

seedless tamarind, lemon-sized ball

1 tbsp Ghee

1 tsp mustard seeds

1 tsp cumin seeds

1 tbsp whole black peppercorns

½ tsp fenugreek seeds

15 fresh curry leaves

1 small bunch of cilantro, 10–15 stalks, leaves and stems

½ tsp turmeric

½ tsp any red chili powder of your choice

1–2 green chilies

4 garlic flakes, with skin-roughly pounded

1 tsp grated jaggery

salt

Cookware:
heavy bottom, 2 quart saucepan with fitting lid

big bowl

small skillet

In South India it is believed that a well made Rasam will actually make you feel satiated and energetic on a slow, hot summer day.

Tamarind is the fruit of the plant Tamarindus Indica. It is very sour and has a sweet after taste if you sip water while eating some. Only the pulp is used extensively in Indian cooking and all over South East Asia. It has been a key ingredient in the international brands of worcestershire and other sauces for years now.

Soak the tamarind in a bowl with 1½ cups of very hot water. When the water is cool enough to touch, mash the tamarind for 3–4 minutes, extracting every bit of its flavor. Do not discard the pulp; leave it in the water for now.

In a large, deep saucepan, take 4 cups of water. Do not turn the heat on yet. Add the thick tamarind extract to the water.

In the bowl with the leftover tamarind pulp, add another cup of water and mash it again. You will get the second extract of tamarind. Add this also to the water and first extract in the larger saucepan and discard the pulp.

In a separate bowl, add the stems and a few leaves of the cilantro, 8–9 curry leaves and a dash of salt and mash this mixture for 2–3 minutes. Add it to the tamarind water in the saucepan. Add the turmeric, red chili powder, green chilies, a little more salt, coarsely ground black pepper and 2 flakes of garlic – pounded with skin on.

Bring the rasam to a boil on high heat. Lower heat to medium and allow it to cook on a rolling boil for 7–9 minutes.

In a small skillet, heat 1 tbsp Ghee. Add the fenugreek seeds. When they turn a shade darker, add mustard seeds, cumin seeds, curry leaves, dried red chilies, and 2 more garlic flakes, with skin on. Stir for a minute or less.

Add this sizzling mix to the rasam that should be simmering on the side. Add the jaggery. Allow it to boil for 2 minutes more. Let it stand for 5 minutes before serving.

Bhindi Stir fried okra

Okra is a versatile and nutritious vegetable. Some like it soft and gooey in a stew, like in a Southern style Gumbo. And some like it sautéed with spices, like this version of okra. It is one of our favourite dishes and makes a great side on a hot summer day!

Serves
4 Medium Portions

1½ lbs young, tender okra

2 green chilies

15 fresh curry leaves

1 tsp cumin seeds

½ tsp mustard seeds

¼ tsp fenugreek seeds

½ tsp asafetida

1 tbsp fresh, roasted coriander powder

1 tsp fresh, roasted cumin powder

1 tsp turmeric powder

1 tsp raw-mango powder (*amchur*)

½ tsp red chili powder

¼ tsp sugar

salt

¼ cup cilantro

3 tbsp Ghee

Wash and dry the okra thoroughly (even slight moisture can make them very gooey and difficult to cook). Cut them into approximately 1 inch pieces, discarding the tops and extreme tips.

In a heavy wok or skillet, heat 2 tbsp Ghee. Add the mustard seeds and allow them to pop. Lower heat to medium and add the salt, cumin seeds, fenugreek seeds and asafetida. Stir for 10 seconds and add the curry leaves and green chilies.

A few seconds later, add the cut okra. Stir on high heat for 2–3 minutes.

Lower heat again and allow the okra to cook until tender. Stir constantly to make sure that the okra and the spices do not burn. Do not cover as the lid will collect moisture and the condensation may drip onto the okra.

Only stir every few minutes on medium to low heat. Once the okra is tender and cooked through, add the last tbsp of Ghee and mix on medium to high heat. Then add all the powdered spices, salt, and sugar. Stir on medium to high heat for a minute more. Add the cilantro. Check the seasoning and add more salt if needed. Take it off the heat and serve immediately.

Cookware:
heavy bottom wok or Indian *kadhai*

Kitchen Tip: *When cooking vegetables in Indian spices, without any water or liquid, a little extra Ghee always adds a celebratory note to the dish! So if you are cooking for yourself, go easy on the Ghee – but for your guests, remember to add a little extra.*

Naan Flatbread with all-purpose flour

Serves
5–6 medium Naans

2½ cups sifted all purpose
flour
½ tsp baking soda (soda
bicarb)
½ tsp salt
1 tsp fine sugar
2 tbsp Ghee
½ cup yoghurt
Ghee as required
warm water

Optional ingredients
1 tsp nigella seeds

Cookware:
An adjustable gas-flame
Tawa with a handle, a light,
iron griddle that is flat or
slightly concave.

Unlike the restaurant version, this recipe does not use any yeast. Traditionally Naans were made in deep clay ovens called Tandoors. They are a popular form of bread that traveled through Central Persia to Northern India during the Mughal period.

Today Naans are available all over the world in the freezer section of most grocery stores. In case of leftovers, make them crisp in a toaster and serve with your favorite dip!

Keep ½ cup sifted all purpose flour aside for later use. Take 2 cups of sifted all purpose flour, salt, baking soda and the sugar in a large mixing bowl. Using your hand, mix it well. Add 2 tbsp Ghee and mix into the flour. Add the yoghurt and mix again. Adding very little warm water at a time, bring the flour mix together into a soft dough. Knead this for 8 to 10 minutes until pliable. Cover with a damp cloth and rest the dough in the same bowl.

After 4–5 hours, the dough will have risen slightly. Grease your hand with a few drops of oil and knead it again for 5–7 minutes. Divide the dough into 5–6 equal portions. Put the *Tawa* or iron griddle on the stove-top. With the help of the dry flour kept aside, roll out the naan into a round or oval shape.

Usually a naan is 5–6 inches in diameter. Do not make the naans too thin. 1/8th of an inch in thickness is good. Sprinkle nigella seeds on one side only. Roll it lightly, to secure the seeds from falling off while cooking. Flip the rolled naan on one hand and apply water with a brush, on the plain side.

Carefully place the naan, water-side down, on the hot *Tawa*. The nigella should be visible to you, with the water coated side on the *Tawa*. Lower heat to medium and wait until a few bubbles appear on the dough.

Now flip the *Tawa* with the help of the handle. The naan will stick to the *Tawa* because of the water. Hold it 1½ inches above the flame, adjusting the heat so that the naan cooks through. Once brown spots appear on the side you are holding against the open flame, the naan is cooked through.

With the help of a spatula, remove the naan to a serving plate. Brush melted Ghee on the side which has the nigella seeds. Serve hot.

Sheera Sweet semolina dessert

Serves
5–6 Medium Portions

1 cup semolina

1 cup Ghee

1 cup milk

1 cup water

1 cup sugar

¾ tsp cardamom powder

1 tbsp small brown raisins

1 tbsp almonds, sliced

few strands of saffron,
soaked in a tbsp of warm milk

Cookware:

small sauce pan

heavy bottom wok or deep
skillet

Sweet Sheera is often made as an evening snack. When making it for informal occasions, you can adjust the quantity of Ghee and use only half the recommended amount. This version of Sheera is for festive occasions and made on certain auspicious days.

This recipe is loaded with goodness in the form of semolina, raisins, almonds and Ghee. Make it on a day that demands high physical activity; you will be sure to work it off in a couple of hours.

Mix the water and milk in a saucepan and allow it to heat slowly. Heat the Ghee in a heavy wok. Fry the raisins until plump, then drain and reserve. Fry the almonds until aromatic and slightly colored, then drain and reserve.

Carefully add the semolina to the remaining Ghee and roast until slightly pink and aromatic.

The milk and water mixture should be almost at boiling point while the semolina has roasted. Take it off the heat.

Lower the heat under the wok to minimum. Pour the hot milk and water mixture, very carefully and slowly, into the roasting semolina. The semolina will splutter, splash and react to the hot liquid.

Keep stirring in a continuous motion while pouring the milk, making sure no lumps are formed. Keep the heat very low once you've added the milk. Add the sugar on top of the mixture. Do not stir, let the sugar dissolve slowly.

Cover and steam for 2–3 minutes. Open and stir well, mixing the sugar, semolina and Ghee. The milk and water should have evaporated, and the Sheera will now have a moist but crumbly texture.

Add the raisins, almonds and cardamom powder. With a fork, fluff the Sheera, making sure the sugar is well incorporated into the mix. Add the soaked saffron and milk. Fluff again and keep covered.

Should be served warm.

Fall Menu

Channa Daal Khichadi
Rice with Bengal gram lentils

Panchmel Daal
Medley of five lentils

Jeera Rice
Cumin rice

Rasam
Spicy broth with tomato

Aloo Gobi
Potatoes with cauliflower

Methi Thepla
Bread with fresh fenugreek leaves

Kheer
Rice and milk dessert

Channa Daal Khichadi Rice with bengal gram lentils

This is an all time favorite, but tastes exceptional when the days have just started getting a little cooler and the evenings a little longer. A perfect Khichadi for the Fall, the combination of whole spices with the Channa Daal is nourishing and heartwarming.

Serves
4 Medium Portions

¾ cup brown rice

½ cup *channa daal* (split Bengal Gram lentils)

3 tbsp Ghee

1 small onion, finely chopped

1 large or 2 small, juicy, ripe tomatoes

½ tsp whole black peppercorns

½ tsp black pepper powder

2 inch piece cinnamon stick

4 green cardamoms

6 cloves

2 bay leaves

1 tsp cumin seeds

2 dried red chilies

2 inch piece of fresh ginger root, grated

½ tsp turmeric

¼ tsp asafetida

small bunch cilantro

salt

1 lime

Cookware:
 2 quart heavy bottom saucepan with lid

Wash the rice and lentils together and soak in 2 cups of water for an hour. In a deep saucepan, heat 2 tbsp Ghee on high. Lower the heat to medium.

Add the whole spices : cinnamon, cardamoms, cloves, bay leaves, whole black pepper and dried red chilies. Add the cumin seeds, allow them to splutter for a few seconds. Add the asafetida, stir. Increase the heat to medium.

Add the finely chopped onions. Stir fry them with the spices for a few minutes, until golden brown. Add the grated ginger root and fry for 2 minutes more.

Drain the water from the soaked rice and lentils, and add it to the sizzling onions. Add the turmeric and black pepper powder and stir gently for 2 minutes.

Add 4 cups of hot water. Add salt and diced tomatoes, stir gently. Add half the cilantro and bring the mix to a rolling boil.

Allow the Khichadi to boil on high heat for 2 minutes. Lower the heat and simmer covered for 30 minutes, stirring once or twice only. If the water dries up too fast, add another cup of boiling water – this may happen depending on the quality of brown rice being used.

Once the rice is very soft, take the Khichadi off from the heat. Add 1 tbsp of Ghee and garnish with the remaining cilantro. Serve steaming hot with wedges of lime and your favorite pickle.

Kitchen Tip:
Remember to cook this Khichadi on a low and slow heat. This will ensure a great texture. Both brown rice and channa daal are ingredients that cannot be rushed.

Panchmel Daal Medley of five lentils

Serves 4
Medium Portions

Panch in North India means five. This medley probably originated a century ago when some housewife had a handful of these lentils left over at the base of each individual receptacle.

¼ cup each *daal: toor* (pigeon peas) yellow mung, *masoor* (red lentil), *channa* (Bengal gram), *urad* (white lentil)

3 tbsp Ghee

1 tsp cumin seeds

1 tsp mustard seeds

1 tbsp freshly grated ginger root

3–4 garlic cloves, grated or ground

1 small onion finely chopped

2 tomatoes finely chopped

5–6 curry leaves

¾ tsp turmeric

1 tbsp coriander powder

1 tsp cumin powder

1 tsp red chili powder

½ tsp *garam masala* (pg 91)

1 tsp dried fenugreek leaves, crushed

1 slit green chili

½ cup cilantro leaves

1 tbsp lemon juice

Cookware:

Two heavy bottom saucepans with fitting lids

Wash and soak the lentils together for an hour. Cook the soaked lentils in 3 cups of fresh water until done. In a separate, heavy bottom saucepan or deep wok, heat 2 tbsp Ghee. Add the mustard seeds – allow them to pop. Lower the heat.

Add the cumin and allow it to turn a shade darker. Add the curry leaves, ginger and garlic. Stir for a minute and add the finely cut onions. Stir until the onions are pink, adjusting the heat accordingly. Add the turmeric, cumin, coriander powders. Stir for a minute. Add the tomatoes, cook on medium high, stirring constantly.

The Ghee will begin to separate. Add the red chili powder and ½ tsp Garam Masala. After another minute or two, add the cooked lentils. Add some water to adjust the consistency of the lentils if needed.

This is a fairly hearty and thick soup, so do not add too much water. Add salt and check seasoning. Add the crushed, dried fenugreek leaves. Add the slit green chili and half the cilantro.

Cover and cook on low heat for another 6 minutes. Garnish with the remaining cilantro and lemon juice. Serve hot with steaming rice, millet-*chapatis* or by itself.

 Kitchen Tip:

Every lentil has a different consistency when cooked. Urad daal (black gram) is more viscous compared to channa daal (Bengal gram) which tends to retain its shape and bite even when well cooked.

Jeera Rice Cumin rice

Cumin is called Jeera in Hindi. It is a very popular form of making rice that adds a festive touch to the most ordinary meals. Add a dash of turmeric when you add the salt and the Jeera rice will turn a delicious golden, resembling the restaurant version of itself.

Serves
3–4 Medium Portions

1 cup long grain white Basmati rice

1 tsp cumin seeds

2 tbsp Ghee

salt

Optional Ingredients:

1 inch piece cinnamon

2 green cardamoms

1 bay leaf

4 cloves

Cookware:
A 2 quart, heavy bottom saucepan with tight fitting lid

Wash and drain the rice half an hour before you plan to cook it.

In a deep and heavy saucepan, heat 2 tbsp Ghee.

Add the optional spices (if using), swirl them around in the Ghee. After a few seconds, add the cumin seeds. Allow them to splutter, making sure to regulate the heat so that the cumin does not burn.

Add the washed and drained Basmati rice. Stir gently without breaking the delicate grains of rice. Add 2 cups of water and salt. Stir lightly.

On high heat, bring the rice and water mixture to a rolling boil. After 2–3 minutes of boiling, bring the heat to low and cook uncovered until the water has almost dried out. This usually takes 7–8 minutes.

Lower heat a little more and use a lid to cover the pan. Cook until the water is completely dry and the rice is cooked, another 4-5 minutes. Put off the heat and leave partially covered for 5 minutes before serving.

 Kitchen Tip:

The optional whole spices add a different dimension of flavor to Jeera rice and make it even better. Cumin tends to burn very fast, so make sure that the Ghee is hot, but not smoking when you add it.

Rasam Spicy broth with Tomato

Tomato Rasam is a favorite in South India. Although tomatoes were brought to the Indian sub-continent by Portuguese traders in the late 1400s, they have become such an intrinsic part of Indian cuisine that we just cannot imagine it without them.

Serves
4 Large Portions

4 large, juicy, ripe and sour tomatoes, diced small
1 cup cilantro leaves and tender stalks, rinsed and cut fine
15 fresh curry leaves
1 tbsp coriander seeds
1¼ tbsp black peppercorns
½ tsp cumin seeds
3 flakes garlic
2 tbsp *toor daal* (pigeon pea lentils), soaked overnight, cooked in 1 cup water and mashed thoroughly
½ tsp turmeric powder
salt
1 tsp grated jaggery
3 dry red chilies

Cookware:
large mixing bowl
3 quart heavy bottom saucepan
mortar pestle or spice grinder

In a large mixing bowl, mix all the diced tomatoes, 10 fresh curry leaves, ¾ cup cut cilantro, leaves and stems, a little salt. Mash this with your hand, breaking down the tomato pieces and cilantro as you go along. Should take at least 5–7 minutes of mashing all the ingredients to a thick homogeneous mixture.

Put this mix into a heavy bottom saucepan with 4 cups warm water. Bring to a boil on low to medium heat.

While it is heating, coarsely grind the coriander seeds, 1 tbsp peppercorns; ¼ tsp cumin seeds and 2 flakes of garlic. Add this mix to the tomatoes heating in the saucepan. Let it come to a boil on medium heat.

Add the cooked and mashed *toor daal*. Simmer for 10 to 15 minutes on low heat.

Meanwhile prepare the tempering: crush the remaining ¼ tsp cumin, peppercorns, 1 flake of garlic and 5 curry leaves in a mortar pestle. Grind the mixed spices coarsely, just pounding them a few times to release the flavors.

After 15 minutes, heat 1 tbsp of Ghee separately in a small skillet. Add the mixture from the mortar pestle to the hot Ghee.

Swirl the mix for a few seconds on high heat, without letting it burn. Add it to the simmering Tomato Rasam. Let it boil gently for 2 minutes more and take off from the heat. Allow the Rasam to stand for 5 minutes before serving.

Kitchen Tip: *Some like rasam strained through a sieve, while others enjoy it with the pieces of tomato. Either way, this lip-smacking, spicy broth makes an excellent soup on a cold Fall evening.*

Aloo Gobi Potatoes with cauliflower

There's something about potatoes and cauliflower cooked with Ghee and Indian spices that everyone just loves. In India, aloo gobi rolled in chapatis is a favorite packed lunch. When served with rice and lentils, it's the most satisfying, complete meal.

Serves
4 Medium Portions

1½ cups cauliflower florets, cut small

1 cup potatoes, cubed in a similar size

2 tbsp Ghee

1 tsp cumin seeds

¼ tsp asafetida

10 fresh curry leaves

1 tbsp grated ginger

1 tsp crushed garlic

½ tsp turmeric powder

½ tsp black salt

1 tbsp coriander powder

1 tsp cumin powder

½ tsp red chili powder

1 green chili

½ cup finely cut cilantro

juice of 1 lime

1 tsp *garam masala* (pg 91)

1 medium onion

1 large tomato (optional)

salt

Cookware:
large wok or skillet

In a wok, heat ½ tbsp of Ghee. Add the cauliflower florets and stir fry on very high heat. They should get a few brown flecks and just a little tender. Remove and reserve.

Add another ½ tbsp of Ghee and fry the cubed potatoes. They should also get slightly colored, but not burned. Let the potatoes cook all the way through, adjusting the heat as you go along. Remove and reserve.

In the same wok, heat the remaining 1 tbsp Ghee. Add the cumin seeds and very quickly add the asafetida and curry leaves. Lower the heat; stir for a few seconds. Add the grated ginger, crushed garlic, green chili. Stir fry for one minute, increasing the heat slightly. Make sure the mix does not burn. Add the onions and stir until a dark pink. do not let them become too caramelized. Add salt to cook down the onions.

Add the turmeric, coriander and red chili powders. Add half the Garam Masala. After a good stir, add the tomato and stir on high heat for 2 minutes.

Lower the heat and cover the pan. Allow the tomatoes to cook down and become mushy. When the Ghee separates from the mixture, stir well and add the half cooked cauliflower, half the cilantro and the cooked potatoes.

Lower heat and cover. Allow the cauliflower to cook for another 2–3 minutes. Add the remaining Garam Masala and black salt. Check the seasoning. Add the remaining cilantro and lime juice. Give it one last stir and take it off the heat.

Methi Thepla Bread with fresh fenugreek leaves

These amazingly tasty breads stay fresh and make great picnic food. Have them as a snack or take them along on an overnight journey.

Serves
6 Methi Theplas

1 ½ cups whole wheat flour (fine ground for best results)

4 tbsp chickpea flour

1 cup fresh fenugreek leaves, with a few tender stalks, discard thicker and fibrous stalks

1 tsp coriander seed powder

1 tsp cumin seed powder

½ tsp whole cumin seeds

¼ tsp carom seeds (ajwain)

½ tsp turmeric powder

½ tsp asafetida

1 tsp jaggery, grated or crumbled

1 green chili, minced

1 tsp fresh ginger, grated

salt

2–3 tbsp yogurt

Ghee, as required

Cookware:

large mixing bowl or platter

Tawa: light-weight iron griddle with wooden handle

light and slim rolling pin

small round rolling board

flat wooden or metal spatula

Wash and chop the fenugreek leaves and green chilies as fine as possible. Grate or grind the ginger.

In a large, wide mouthed bowl add all the dry ingredients: whole wheat flour, chickpea flour, salt and spice powders and mix well. Add the chopped fenugreek leaves and gently fold in. Add the yoghurt, jaggery, ginger paste and 1 tbsp of melted Ghee. Combine all the ingredients to make a dough.

Add a few tbsp of hot water if needed – to get a fairly firm dough.

Rest the dough for 20 minutes on the kitchen counter top (do not refrigerate).

After 20 minutes – make a long roll of the dough and divide into 6 equal portions (approximately the size of a golf ball). With the help of a small plate of whole wheat flour for dusting – roll out thin disks of the dough and cook on a hot *Tawa* or iron griddle.

Take your time, do not rush, dip each ball of dough in the dry wheat flour and roll, constantly turning the disk to maintain its round shape. This takes a bit of practice, but the fenugreek *Theplas* will still taste heavenly, no matter the shape.

Always be aware of the heat. If the griddle is too hot, lower the heat so that the *Theplas* do not burn. Once brown spots have appeared on both sides and 3 minutes have elapsed, pour ¼ tsp Ghee on both sides and cook for another few seconds while pressing down gently with the help of a flat wooden or metal spatula.

Stack them on top of each other, in a box or on a plate, lined with a clean kitchen towel. Serve with mixed vegetables and a raita of your choice.

Kheer Rice and milk dessert

Serves
4 Small Portions

2 tbsp Ghee

4 tbsp rice, washed and drained

3½ cups whole milk

2 or 3 tbsp sugar

handful of small light-brown raisins

handful of almonds, sliced

seeds only, from 4 green cardamom, crushed

6 or 7 strands of saffron, soaked in 2 tablespoons warm milk

Cookware:
2 quart, heavy bottom saucepan

small skillet to fry the raisins and nuts

small bowl to soak saffron in milk

Kheer is known as Payasam in South India. The raisins and almonds fried in Ghee and added at the end is what makes this dessert irresistible.

The very same recipe can be used with whole-grain millets like Jowar (Sorghum), Samo (Barnyard Millet) and even Daliya (Bulgur or broken wheat). The cooking time may vary. Rice cooks quickly, while Jowar takes much longer. Just remember to check the time it will take you to cook a different grain in milk.

Add the washed and drained rice to the 2 cups whole milk in a heavy saucepan. Add 1 cup of warm water to the mix. Cook on a medium to low heat until rice is fully cooked and a little mushy.

If the milk evaporates too fast, be prepared to add another cup of milk.

Add the crushed cardamom and sugar and keep stirring on low heat until the sugar is dissolved. Reduce the heat to minimum.

Check consistency, this Kheer can be thick or thin as desired, so adjust it with milk or a little hot water.

In a small skillet, heat 2 tbsp Ghee. Fry the raisins until plump, drain and add them to the Kheer. Raisins swell and become bigger when fried in Ghee but they also burn easily so be careful at this stage. In the same Ghee, fry the almonds until well roasted.

Add the almonds, along with any Ghee leftover in the skillet, to the Kheer. Add the soaked saffron with the milk. Take off from the heat and allow the Kheer to stand for 5-7 minutes before serving.

Kitchen Tip: *Alternatively, cook the milk down, to ¾ of its original amount. Add the sugar and cardamom, mix well and then add the grains which have been separately cooked.*

Winter Menu

Jowar Khichadi
Spiced sorghum millet with vegetables

Kaali Daal
Black (Urad) lentils with skin

Methi Chawal
Rice with fresh fenugreek leaves

Rasam
Spicy broth with pepper

Baby Potatoes
With peanuts and jaggery

Bajra Rotis
Bread with pearl millet flour

Ragi Dosa
Crepes with finger millet flour

Dates and Dry Fruit Bites
Dessert roll

Jowar Khichadi Spiced sorghum millet with vegetables

Serves
4 Medium Portions

1 cup whole Jowar

½ each: red, green and yellow bell peppers, finely chopped

2 tbsp Ghee

1 tsp cumin

1–2 green chilies, cut fine

6 fresh curry leaves

¼ tsp turmeric

¼ tsp asafetida

½ tsp each: cumin and coriander powders

¼ cup finely cut cilantro

juice of half a lemon

Cookware:
2 quart heavy bottom saucepan with fitting lid

heavy bottom wok or skillet

Jowar is a power packed millet. It has protein, iron and calcium and also policosanols that seem to help keep cholesterol levels in check. Nutritious and warm in nature, it is a staple food in rural India.

Also known as Sorghum, it is ground to a fine flour and used to make breads or chapatis which are baked on hot iron griddles. A Jowar chapati, slathered with Ghee and served with a steaming hot lentil is also a wonderfully nutritious winter lunch.

As a Khichadi with vegetables of your choice, Jowar can be a complete food, and is a perfect meal for gluten-free diets.

Soak the Jowar in 3 cups of water overnight.

In a saucepan, cook the rinsed and drained Jowar through with 2 cups of fresh water. Bring it to a boil on high heat, then reduce and let it simmer on low heat for 40 minutes or more.

If needed, add ½ cup of boiling water after 15 minutes of cooking. Jowar will never become as tender as rice. It is a tough grain and will remain crunchy and chewy, and needs at least 45 minutes to cook well.

In a heavy wok, heat 2 tbsp Ghee on high and then lower the heat. Add cumin, sauté for a few seconds, until a shade darker. Add green chilies, asafetida, curry leaves and salt.

After a minute, add the finely chopped bell peppers. Sauté for 2 minutes.

Add ¼ tsp turmeric, ¼ tsp each: cumin and coriander powders and a dash of red chili powder. Add the cooked Jowar along with its cooking liquid. Lower heat and simmer, partially covered, until all the moisture has dried out. Garnish with finely cut cilantro and lemon juice.

Kaali Daal Black urad lentils with skin

Serves
4 Large Portions

1 cup whole black *urad daal* (with skin) – soaked overnight

1 medium onion, cut fine

1–2 medium tomatoes, cut fine or pureed in a blender

1–2 green chilies

2 tsp *garam masala* (pg 91)

1 tsp freshly grated ginger

1 tbsp ginger-garlic paste

salt

4 tbsp heavy whipping cream

1 tbsp coriander powder

1 tsp cumin powder

1 tsp raw-mango powder

cilantro to garnish (optional)

4 tbsp Ghee

½ cup red kidney beans known as *Rajma* in Hindi (soaked along with the black lentil, *optional*)

Cookware:

deep, heavy 3 quart saucepan

large iron skillet or wok

Northern India is dotted with small, rustic places to stop and have a quick bite whilst driving between cities. These hole-in-the-wall eateries are called 'dhaabas' and have always been patronized by truck drivers and tourist buses. One of the favorite entrées on the menu in a typical dhaaba is Kaali-daal.

In Hindi, kaali refers to black and daal to lentils, hence, this is "black-lentils." With different names in different languages, black-skinned urad is actually from the genus Vigno Mungo.

Usually served with hot Naans slathered with more Ghee!

Boil the soaked lentils (and red kidney beans, if using them), in fresh water with salt and 1 tsp of freshly grated ginger until cooked. This could take an hour or more in a saucepan.

The water level should always be a couple of inches above the lentils. Keep adding little hot water if it evaporates too fast. Once the lentils are fully cooked and can be mashed if pressed with the back of a ladle, stop adding any more water.

In a separate skillet or wok, heat 3 tbsp Ghee. Add onions and a pinch of salt. Fry the onions until dark pink or golden. Add the ginger-garlic paste and cook for 2–3 minutes. Add cumin, coriander and 1 tsp *Garam Masala*.

Stir for a minute and then add the tomatoes. Stir on medium to high heat until the tomatoes are mushy and the Ghee separates. Add the boiled lentils along with its liquid to this mix.

Stir and simmer for 10–15 minutes, until well incorporated and fragrant. Mash some of the lentils and red kidney beans against the side of the wok to thicken the soup.

Lower heat to minimum and add the heavy whipping cream, reserving 2 tbsp for the final garnish. Add 1 tsp Garam Masala. Check salt, chili, sourness and adjust. For extra sourness, add ½ tsp dry mango powder. Garnish with 1 tbsp of hot Ghee, fresh cilantro and a swirl of heavy whipping cream.

Methi Chawal Rice with fresh fenugreek leaves

Serves
4 Medium Portions

This aromatic rice is delicious by itself, and even better when served with a mixed vegetable side dish or plain yoghurt.

1 cup washed and drained white Basmati rice

1 cup fresh fenugreek leaves (*methi*) washed and roughly cut

2 green chilies, slit or finely cut

¾ tsp cumin seeds

1 tbsp coriander powder

1 tsp cumin powder

1 small onion finely chopped

1 medium tomato finely chopped

5 garlic flakes, finely chopped or crushed

salt

1 tsp turmeric powder

7 whole black peppercorns

2 tbsp Ghee

1 potato, diced (optional)

Cookware:
mesh sieve
2 quart heavy bottom saucepan with fitting lid

Wash and drain the rice in a mesh sieve. Let it stand for a minimum of 10 minutes before cooking. In a heavy saucepan, take 2 tbsp Ghee. Heat the Ghee on high and then lower the heat. Add cumin seeds and whole black peppercorns. After a few seconds, add green chilies, garlic and salt, stir for 10 seconds.

Add the finely chopped onions and stir fry for 3–4 minutes, until golden brown.. Add the fenugreek leaves and stir on medium to high heat until some of the moisture dries out and the Ghee separates. Add turmeric, coriander and cumin powders.

After 1 minute, add the chopped tomatoes. Stir for 2 minutes and allow the tomatoes to soften slightly. Add the washed rice and stir very gently, taking great care not to break the delicate Basmati rice kernels.

After 2–3 minutes, the mix should be well fried. Add 2 cups warm water and the potato pieces, if using. Bring to a boil on high heat. Check salt, add some if necessary.

Lower the heat, and cook without a lid until the water is no longer above the level of the rice. At this stage, cover the pan with a tight fitting lid and cook until all the water is absorbed. Make sure the heat is very low, or the base may burn.

After 5 minutes, fluff the rice, with the help of a fork. All the water should have dried up by now. Take it off the heat and allow it to stand, partially covered, for 5 minutes before serving.

Kitchen Tip: *There are mixed views on whether one should fluff Basmati rice during the cooking process, or not. If you feel the need to stir the rice while it's cooking, use a fork and work with a light hand.*

Rasam Spicy broth with pepper

Rasam is a fiery hot, spicy broth that makes a great side with any kind of meal.
The spices in Rasam ignite the digestive fire – Agni, and help us metabolize food quicker and
more efficiently. If you cannot handle pepper or the other spices, simply skip this Rasam.

Serves
4 Medium Portions

1 tbsp whole black
peppercorns

10–15 fresh curry leaves

2 dry red chilies

½ cup thick tamarind extract
(soak a lime size ball of
seedless tamarind in ½ a cup
of very hot water for half
an hour, and then squeeze it
out, use the pulp to make a
second thinner extract)

½ cup cilantro, both leaves
and tender stems

salt

8 cloves garlic

1 tsp mustard seeds

1 tsp cumin seeds

1 tbsp coriander seeds

1 tbsp Ghee

Cookware:

deep 3 quart saucepan

spice grinder or mortar pestle

small skillet to make the
Tadka (tempering)

Prep all the ingredients and keep them ready. Take the tamarind extract in a deep saucepan. Mix in half the cilantro, with the tender stems and a few curry leaves that have been torn apart to release their fragrance.

Add salt and mix well. Now add 4 cups of water to this and bring it to a boil on medium heat. Lower the heat and add the second extract of the tamarind pulp.

While the Rasam is simmering on low heat, grind the coriander seeds, ¾ tbsp peppercorns, ½ tsp cumin and 4–5 flakes of garlic, to a coarse mixture. Add this to the simmering Rasam. Allow it to stay on low heat for 15–20 minutes, stirring occasionally.

In a mortar-pestle, roughly pound the remaining garlic, 1/2 tsp cumin seeds, peppercorns and curry leaves. In a separate skillet, heat 1 tbsp Ghee. Add the mustard seeds, allow them to pop. Add the dry red chilies, and the mix from the mortar pestle. Stir for half a minute and add it to the simmering Pepper Rasam.

Increase the heat and bring it to a final boil. Take it off the heat. Add the remaining cilantro. Check the salt, add more if required. Serve in bowls with hot, steamed rice or strain some into a glass and drink like a spiced broth.

Baby Potatoes with peanuts and jaggery

**Serves
4 Large Portions**

1½ pounds baby potatoes (or
2 large potatoes)

10–12 fresh curry leaves

½ tsp asafetida

1 tsp cumin seeds

3 tsp white sesame seeds

2 green chilies, cut fine

4 tbsp roasted peanuts

3 tbsp jaggery

1 tbsp freshly grated ginger
root (optional)

1 tsp freshly roasted and
coarsely ground cumin

a dash of hot cayenne
(optional)

salt

¼ cup finely cut cilantro

3 tbsp Ghee

Cookware:
medium saucepan
large wok

An all time favorite of those who have tried this recipe, it is delicious served hot or at room temperature. It pairs well with a simple lentil soup and steamed rice. Or does equally well with a hot griddle-baked bread, like the chapati.

Boil the potatoes until done (if using organic baby potatoes – leave the skin on to retain the nutrients). Cut the potatoes into halves. If using larger potatoes, cut into bite sized cubes and boil.

Heat Ghee in a wok or large skillet. Add the cumin seeds and asafetida and lower heat to medium. Quickly add the sesame seeds, cut green chilies, curry leaves and grated ginger. Stir for a few seconds and add the cooked baby potatoes. Increase heat and stir fry for a minute.

Crush the peanuts lightly with a rolling pin or in a mortar-pestle. Add the cumin powder, peanuts and jaggery. Stir on high heat for 2 or 3 minutes. Check and adjust the salt. For more chili-heat, add a dash of hot cayenne pepper. Lower heat and do not stir.

Allow a few potatoes and peanuts to caramelize with the jaggery. Once a few pieces of potatoes are brown and all the ingredients are well mixed, take off from heat and garnish with cilantro.

Bajra Rotis Bread with pearl millet flour

These Bajra Rotis are best eaten while hot and fresh. They pair well with all kinds of pickles and raitas, but also make an excellent snack with a hot cup of chai.

Serves
8 Small Bajra Rotis

2 cups *Bajra*, Pearl Millet flour

½ a small onion, very finely cut or grated

1 green chili, finely cut

¼ cup cilantro

½ tsp pepper powder

salt

Ghee as required

Cookware:

large mixing bowl or platter

Tawa: light-weight iron griddle with wooden handle

light and slim rolling pin

small round rolling board or any smooth surface

flat wooden or metal spatula

Heat 2 cups of water to just about boiling point. In a large, fairly flat bowl or platter, take the Bajra flour and add all the ingredients except the hot water and Ghee.

Make a well in the center and add very little hot water. Carefully put the dry ingredient mix over the hot water and start bringing it all together to form a dough.

Use a spoon if the water is too hot initially. After it has cooled slightly, bring it together with your hand. This dough tends to get sticky. Add just enough water to bring it all together. Make a firm and smooth dough.

There is no need to rest this dough at all, since Bajra is a millet and has no gluten. Heat an iron griddle *Tawa* or a skillet. Put a few drops of Ghee on the *Tawa* or skillet and wipe clean with a paper towel. Break the dough into small portions and using both your palms, shape into small discs of 1/8th of an inch thick.

Put it on the well heated *Tawa*, only turn after 2 minutes. Cook the discs patiently on medium heat for at least 3–5 minutes, pressing down every once in a while and turning them over when needed.

The final Bajra Roti has brown spots and is fully cooked through after 5 minutes. While it is still on the griddle, drizzle Ghee on the surface, press down, flip and add a little more Ghee on the other side too. Remove and reserve on a plate until all the Rotis are done. Store in a box lined with a paper towel or foil sheet. Serve with a pickle or a raita of your choice.

Ragi Dosa Crepes with finger millet flour

Serves
4 Small Portions

1 cup ragi flour

¼ cup all purpose flour

2 tbsp rice flour

¼ cup *urad daal* (white lentils)

7 whole fenugreek seeds

salt

Ghee as required

Optional ingredients:

1 small onion

1 green chili minced

4–5 fresh curry leaves

¼ cup cilantro – all cut as finely as possible

½ tsp whole cumin seeds

Cookware:

mixing bowl

flat *Dosa-Tawa*

light iron griddle like a crepe iron skillet with a handle

bowl shaped ladle to pour and spread the batter

Ragi or finger millet is a rich source of protein and calcium. The flour is used in several recipes, including porridge, pancakes, breads and puddings. Because of its nutritional value, Ragi is given to growing children and convalescing adults all over India.

Millets are a great source of nutrition and have been a part of the human diet much before wheat or rice came to be. Archaeologists have found evidence of millets in many research sites all over the world.

Wash the *urad daal*, add the whole fenugreek seeds and soak them in 2 cups of water for 4 hours. Drain the water and grind the *urad daal* and fenugreek seeds with very little fresh water. It should be a fine but thick batter.

In a large mixing bowl, add the ground *urad daal*, ragi flour, rice flour, and salt. Keep this mix covered in a warm place overnight.

The next morning, stir the batter lightly. If using the optional ingredients, add them now. Heat the *Dosa-Tawa* (or a flat iron griddle) on high for 5 minutes, then reduce heat to medium. Alternatively, use a large, flat crepe pan. Take a ladle full of the batter, pour it in the center of the lightly greased *Tawa*. Starting from the center, move the ladle lightly, with firm circular motions. Spread the batter in an outward movement as thin as possible with the back of the ladle.

Make a circular crepe almost as big as the *Tawa* itself. A few holes may appear initially, but it will get better with practice. Increase the heat to medium high, and drizzle drops of Ghee along the side of the pan and on top of the ragi-dosa. Flip it after 2 minutes and cook for another minute or two. The edges should be a little crisp and the dosa itself turns an appetizing red-brown.

Serve with your favorite pickle or chutney.

 Kitchen Tip: *The trick to making any kind of dosa (Indian crepe) is to heat the flat-iron griddle on very high heat, then cool it slightly to spread the batter, and finally to regulate the heat constantly while it cooks. It takes a few attempts before one gets it right.*

Date and Dry Fruit Bites

Makes 3 Logs,
5 inches in length

Dates are truly nutritious. Although they are 80% sugar, they have protein, potassium and fiber with trace elements of several essential minerals. Dates are like an instant energy food directly from nature.

1½ cups pitted, soft, juicy, organic dates

1 cup mixed nuts (walnuts, hazelnuts, almonds, cashews and macadamia), roasted and coarsely chopped

2–3 tbsp Ghee (depends on how moist the dates are)

¼ cup + 2 tbsp coconut flakes

2 tbsp white poppy seeds

In a heavy bottom wok, heat 1 tbsp Ghee. Add the dates and keep stirring on medium to low heat . After 4–5 minutes, add another tbsp of Ghee. The dates will melt and become a sticky mixture in a few minutes. After 3 minutes, add the chopped nuts. Add the coconut flakes, reserving 2 tbsp.

Bring the mixture together on low heat until it starts leaving the side of the wok. If it feels too dry, add more Ghee, a ¼ tbsp at a time.

The mixture should be homogenous and pliable rather than runny or stiff. Take it off the heat and allow it to cool for 5 minutes.

Cookware:
heavy bottom wok, with handle
flat wooden or ceramic surface
shrink wrap

Roll it into 3 tight and firm logs. Roll the logs in the reserved coconut, coating them evenly. Wrap as tightly and firmly as possible in shrink wrap.

Refrigerate for a couple of hours. Unwrap and roll the logs in the 2 tbsp of poppy seeds. Slice into slim discs and serve.

Kitchen Tip: *Coupled with power-packed fruits and nuts, this is one of the best desserts to have on hand. Make these logs and store in the freezer for a few months. Defrost in the refrigerator a day before you plan to serve them.*

SPICE
BLENDS

Masala is simply a word for spice blends that are
mixed together to enhance the flavors.

One can add masala combinations to anything
just by mixing a handful of ingredients.

Garam Masala A typical Indian spice blend

One 8oz Jar

2 tbsp cumin

2 tbsp coriander

2 tbsp black or brown mustard

1 tbsp fennel seeds

1 tbsp whole black pepper

3 tbsp star anise

3 tbsp mace (flower of the nutmeg plant)

dried bay leaves

6 dried red chilies (can be increased or decreased by preference)

1 tsp cloves

1 tsp whole green cardamoms

4 one inch pieces of cinnamon

2 black cardamom

Cookware:

heavy skillet or wok

spice grinder

air-tight glass jar for storage

Every region in India has its own version of this spice blend. In fact, every household in a given area will have slight variations in the Garam Masala of choice.

Here the word garam means "hot" as in warming. This spice blend ignites the digestive fires.

Roast all the ingredients in an iron skillet over low heat for 3 or 4 minutes.

Remove to a cool plate as leaving them in a hot iron skillet may cause them to burn. Grind to a fine powder, once the mix is cool. Store in an air-tight glass jar.

This has a very long shelf life, though there is no substitute for freshly ground Garam Masala. We suggest you make a small amount every once in a while.

Chaat Masala

One 6oz Jar

2 tbsp cumin seeds
½ tbsp black peppercorns
2 tbsp dry mango powder
1 tsp black salt
½ tsp regular salt

Cookware:
medium skillet
spice grinder
air-tight glass jar for storage

The ingredients in this spice mix aid digestion and therefore it is liberally sprinkled on many foods, salads, smoothies and even certain fruits.

The simplest recipe to use this spice mix is to blend ½ cup yoghurt, a few ice cubes and ½ cup chilled water, add ½ tsp Chaat Masala and enjoy a lip-smacking summer cooler. Serve this with any Khichadi from the Spring or Summer sections in this book.

Dry roast the cumin and whole black pepper for 2 minutes on a low flame. Grind the cumin and black pepper to a fine powder.

In a bowl, mix all the ingredients including the finely ground powder. Mix and store in a cool dry place.

Chai Masala

One 8oz Jar

¼ cup dry ginger powder
(*saunth/soonth*)

2 one inch pieces of
cinnamon

1 tsp green cardamom seeds

¼ tsp black cardamon seeds

15–20 cloves

1 tbsp black peppercorns

1 tbsp fennel seeds

Cookware:
heavy skillet or wok
spice grinder
air-tight glass jar for storage

This spice blend is excellent as a tea on a cold winter day, or when you are fighting a 'flu. Store this special chai masala or chai spice in an airtight glass bottle.

Grind all the ingredients in a spice grinder except the dry ginger powder. When coarsely ground, add the dry ginger powder and continue grinding until fine.

To use this mix: Add ¼ tsp to boiling water and a tea bag of your choice. Allow it to stand for 2–3 minutes before adding milk and sugar if required.

Sambar Masala A spice blend for lentils

One 16oz Jar

1 cup coriander seeds

¼ tsp asafetida

½ tsp salt

1/8th cup *toor daal* (pigeon-peas)

1/8th cup *channa daal* (split Bengal gram)

1 tsp fenugreek seeds

1 tbsp black peppercorns

10–15 dried red chilies (choose a mild version like Kashmiri chillies)

1 tbsp cumin seeds

2 tsp turmeric powder

Cookware:

heavy skillet or wok

spice grinder

glass jar for storage

This blend stays well if stored in a clean glass jar in a cool and dry pantry. Should be good for at least six months to a year possibly. Although commonly used for lentils, try it with sautéed vegetables too.

Also, please be aware that it will not taste exactly like store bought Sambar powder, since every brand adds or omits certain ingredients. The reason why we prefer our version is because it is not too spicy and always tastes awesome!

Dry roast each ingredient separately, except the turmeric powder and asafetida. After roasting, collect all the ingredients in one bowl and grind into a fine powder in a spice-blender. Add the turmeric powder and asafetida and mix well.

Store in an airtight glass bottle.

PICKLES
& CHUTNEYS

A curated selection of mouthwatering pickles
and chutneys to enjoy with these amazingly
simple Ghee recipes!

Lemon, Ginger, & Fresh Turmeric Pickle

This delicious pickle tastes great with anything. While traditionalists will have a spoonful with hot, fresh Khichadi or chapatis, feel free to experiment with it. Add it to a sandwich, spread a little on your toast, or just toss a spoonful with freshly cooked, steaming rice!

One 16oz Jar

10 organic, juicy lemons, washed and cut into quarters or eight pieces each

¼ cup grated ginger root

¼ cup grated fresh turmeric root

½ cup mustard oil

2 tbsp salt

2 tbsp fennel seeds

1½ tbsp mustard seeds

1 tbsp turmeric powder

2 tbsp red chili powder (optional)

Cookware:

large glass or ceramic, wide mouthed jar or bowl to mix the pickle

small, clean and sterilized glass jars to preserve the pickle in

Put the washed, dried and cut lemon pieces into a big glass or ceramic bowl.

Add salt, cover loosely with a ceramic plate, and keep in a warm, preferably sunny place for 24 hours. This will help the lemons release their moisture.

After 24 hours, add the grated turmeric and ginger. Add the turmeric powder. Grind the mustard seeds to a fine powder and add it to the mix.

Coarsely grind or pulse the fennel seeds and add them too. Add the red chili powder if using. With a sterile and dry metal spoon, mix the ingredients until all the lemon pieces are well coated.

Now pour the mustard oil over the pickle and stir lightly and briefly. The oil should be just at the level of the ingredients. Allow it to settle for a few minutes, only then remove the spoon, just in case you need to mix it again.

Cover it with a loosely fitted saucer, plate or lid, allowing it to breathe. Do not put an airtight lid on it. Keep this bowl or jar in direct sunlight for 3–4 days, stirring just once or twice. This pickle is then ready to eat.

Divide it into smaller jars and refrigerate for a longer shelf life.

Raw Mango Pickle

One 16oz Jar

4 raw mangoes with thin skins, preferably very sour

½ cup red chili powder, use the mild, Kashmiri chili powder if you do not like it too hot

2 tbsp salt

½ tsp asafetida

2 tbsp turmeric powder

room temperature filtered water, as required

Cookware:

sharp knife, chopping board

tall, clear glass or ceramic pickle jar with a wide mouth

Summer in India is 'pickling season'. Almost every household has a secret pickled raw-mango recipe that makes the pickle unique to that family. These recipes were treated like heirlooms and handed down by the elderly women. Strangely, given the same ingredients, the same method, the same weather, the same pickle would taste very different when made by a different person.

Using clean and sterile utensils, cut the raw mangoes with skin into tiny pieces.

Put the mango pieces into a large, wide mouth, glass or ceramic jar.

Sprinkle with salt and toss. Cover loosely and set aside in hot sunlight for an entire day.

After 24 hours, add the spices and salt and give it a good shake.

Now leave this mix in the hot sun again for 2 days. Make sure it is loosely covered to prevent dust particles from settling on it.

It must breathe. Do not use an air tight container. After 2 days, add cool filtered water just until the level of the mango pieces. Leave it for one more day on the table top or in the sun and it will be ready.

Refrigerate for a longer shelf life.

 Kitchen Tip: *If you manage to get this pickle right, you will be making it again and again. It is light, has no oil and adds a spicy, tangy punch to everything, including a salad dressing!*

Cilantro, Green Chili, Mint & Cumin Chutney

One Medium Bowl

1½ cup cilantro leaves and a few tender stalks, washed and roughly chopped

1–2 green chilies

½ cup mint leaves, washed and roughly chopped

¼ inch piece of ginger

1 large garlic flake

1 small piece of onion (optional)

¼ tsp cumin seeds

salt

1 tbsp tamarind extract or juice of half a lemon

1 tsp sugar (optional)

Cookware:
medium sized mixing bowl

blender

glass bowl with lid, to store the chutney

This chutney is best when fresh. However, it keeps well in the refrigerator for a few days. Serve it with dosa, pan fried snacks or use it as a spread in a sandwich. Any which way, it is delicious.

Blend all the ingredients into a smooth chutney without any water if possible.

If using tamarind, add it while grinding. If using lemon juice, add it after all the ingredients have been ground. Add only 1–2 tbsp water if required. Check salt, sugar and chili – adjust if necessary.

Coconut chutney

Makes
One Medium Bowl

1 cup fresh or frozen grated coconut

1 green chili

½ inch piece ginger root

1 tbsp roasted *channa daal* (split Bengal gram)

¼ cup yoghurt (optional)

5–7 stalks fresh cilantro – use the leaves and tender stalks

small teeny bit of seedless tamarind

1 tsp Ghee

½ tsp mustard seeds

¼ tsp cumin seeds

5–6 fresh curry leaves

2 dried red chilies

1 tsp *urad daal* (white lentils)

salt

Cookware:
medium sized mixing bowl
blender
glass bowl with lid, to store the chutney

This chutney is delicious with any kind of Indian crepe or dosa. Try it with the Ragi dosa or even with a simple meal of rice and lentils. Coconut chutney is best had the day it's made. It may not last longer than 2 days in the refrigerator. We suggest you make very small batches of it and finish it as soon as possible.

Blend the coconut, yoghurt, green chilies, roasted *channa daal*, ginger root, tamarind, salt and cilantro to a fine, thick paste.

Use only 1 or 2 tsp water if needed. In a small skillet, heat the Ghee. Add mustard seeds and *urad daal*. Allow the mustard seeds to pop and the *daal* to turn pink.

Lower heat and add cumin seeds, dried red chilies and fresh curry leaves. Swirl for a few seconds and pour over the chutney while it is still sizzling.

Kitchen Tip: *For a vegan version – replace the yoghurt with chilled coconut cream. As a substitute for tamarind – you can add the juice of half a lime. But add this after grinding the chutney – not during the process as you would the tamarind.*

Garlic and Red Chili Chutney

Makes
One Medium Bowl

1 garlic pod, 10 flakes

7 dry red Kashmiri chilies

½ tsp sesame seeds

¼ tsp cumin seeds

½ tsp coarse sea salt

1 tbsp vinegar
or juice of 1 lemon

Cookware:

medium sized mixing bowl

food processor

glass bowl with lid, to store
the chutney

This is usually kept on hand in the refrigerator and is a common go-to chutney. It can be added to a Khichadi, or eaten with a millet or wheat bread (chapati). Or it can also be added to stir fried vegetables just before taking them off the heat.

It is very spicy and tangy and perfect if you love the flavor of garlic. Just a little hint of it is enough!

Soak the red chilies, cumin and sesame seeds in vinegar or lemon juice for an hour. Grind the mixture together.

Check for salt and vinegar. Add if necessary.

 Kitchen Tip: *This chutney keeps well for a few weeks. It can also be added to a stir-fry or to freshly cooked rice to spice things up!*

Contributors

Chitra Martin, *Author*
Chitra enjoyed writing advertising copy for international clients years ago. She moved to Los Angeles in 2008 and now manages a real estate business. At the same time, she pursues a lifelong interest in art and is a school-group Docent at the Getty Center. She has an abiding passion for Indian aesthetics, culture and cuisine.

Susanne Jarchow-Misch, *Art Director and Co-Publisher*
Susanne started making Ghee at home many years ago. She enjoys traveling to India and experimenting with Indian cuisine. She has done the Panchakarma, an Ayurvedic total detoxification and would like to share the inherent and potential benefits of Ghee with you through this book.

Nakul Patel, *Co-Publisher*
Nakul is a Chicago-based entrepreneur in the health and wellness domain. As a founder of Maha Ghee, Nakul is on a mission to reintroduce conscious consumers to the highest standards of this storied and most wholesome of traditional Indian superfoods.

Marisa Paolillo, *Contributor*
Marisa is the chef-owner at Mango Pickle, a contemporary Indian Bistro in Chicago. An avid Ghee user, Marisa is among a handful of culinary professionals exploring the creative possibilities of Ghee in modern-day recipes.

Richard Wright, *Photographer*
Richard is an eclectic photographer whose passions embrace fashion, beauty and celebrity portraiture. He likes to synthesize extreme graphic realism with a traditional, classical sensibility.
www.richardwrightphotography.com

Lauren Allik, *Graphic Designer*
Lauren Allik is a Los Angeles based graphic designer who specializes in print and branding.
www.laurenallik.com

First edition January 2019.

ISBN: 978-0-578-40503-2

Co-Published by
Sansaar
Los Angeles, CA
sansaar@sansaar.co
&
Holy Basil LLC
Chicago, IL
holybasilllc@gmail.com

Printed and bound by JAK Printers Pvt Ltd.
Mumbai, India
jakprinters.com